The Pop-Up Shop Boom
Starting a Temporary Retail Business

Table of Contents

Chapter 1. Introduction

Dive headfirst into the bustling world of pop-up stores with our thrilling Special Report: "The Pop-Up Shop Boom: Starting a Temporary Retail Business." The retail landscape is blooming with vibrant, creative, and innovative business strategies that are shaking up the norm, and no approach is making waves quite like the pop-up shop. This report provides a thrilling ride through the ins and outs of starting your robust venture in the exciting domain of temporary retail. Packed with insightful lessons, proven strategies, and joyful anecdotes from successful entrepreneurs, this report is an absolute must-have! Uncover the secrets of pop-up retailers, fuel your entrepreneurial spirit, and picture yourself unlocking doors to your very own pop-up shop! Whisk yourself away on a business adventure like no other and watch as your retail dreams come to life!

Chapter 2. Understanding the Pop-Up Retail Phenomenon

To wrap your head around the pop-up retail phenomenon, it's essential to first visit the roots of this rapidly expanding strategy. Pop-up retailers, also known as flash retailing, have emerged as a thriving business trend gaining astounding momentum over the past decade. It is a contemporary twist to the classic retail model, where brands set up short-term sales spaces: low-cost, high-energy environments designed to foster a stir and engage customers with 'limited time only' offerings.

2.1. What Drives the Pop-Up Revolution?

There are several key factors fueling the boom of the pop-up economy. One of the driving forces behind this revolution is the evolving expectations of modern consumers. In the age of online shopping, retail-tainment, or creating an entertaining and immersive shopping experience, has been on the rise. Consumers value the thrill of finding unique, limited edition products while being part of a unique shopping experience that pop-ups offer.

Further, the economic recession has made marketers and retailers think out of the box. By creating a pop-up shop, businesses can test a location or a new product line, introduce a new brand or concept, and interact with customers in an entirely different, more personalized manner, all without the long-term commitments and high costs of a permanent commercial lease.

2.2. From Temporary Storefronts to Global Sensation

So, how did temporary shops grow into a global sensation? Many attribute the rise of pop-ups to the economic downturn in the early 2000s. This era saw a rise in vacant retail spaces which could be temporarily leased to generate some cash flow. Businesses quickly started capitalizing on these opportunities. Some of the early adopters of this trend, like fashion brands Comme des Garçons and Target, found that it was a great way to create a lot of buzz around their brand in a short period.

As retail space became more readily available and consumers increasingly sought innovative shopping experiences, the pop-up model spiraled into a global sensation. From LA's flea markets to established brands in London's Covent Garden, pop-up stores are uniting the commercial with the creative, instilling a sense of urgency in consumers everywhere.

Over the years, this model has attracted a diverse group of retailers, including online startups looking to make an offline impact, to high-end fashion brands utilizing pop-up venues as a promotional tool, and even independent artisans eager to reach new audiences. With a broad appeal, the pop-up retail phenomenon has become an essential part of the modern retail toolkit.

2.3. Creating Buzz with Pop-Up Shops

Pop-up shops offer a unique advantage in the world of retail - buzz creation. When executed correctly, pop-ups create a sense of urgency and exclusivity that drives consumer interest and incites immediate action. They are a powerful tool to increase brand visibility, particularly in high foot traffic areas. Moreover, they offer a platform to express the brand's personality, connect with customers, and create lasting, shareable experiences.

Many retailers have clocked onto this and have used pop-up stores as a part of their marketing strategies, focusing not just on sales but also on creating an experience. For instance, online mattress retailer Casper opened pop-up 'nap pods' offering city dwellers a solution to afternoon fatigue and expanding its brand name in a unique, interactive way.

2.4. Embracing Flexibility and Innovation in Retail

The pop-up model's real power lies in its flexible, short-term nature, allowing businesses to reap benefits without major commitments. Companies can experiment with new avenues, test consumer reactions, and harness real-time feedback to make immediate adjustments, fostering an environment of innovation.

2.5. Conclusion

Overall, the rise of pop-up retail is a strong indicator of how the retail industry has evolved to meet ever-changing consumer preferences. They epitomize the spirit of business innovation: quick-response, short term, low-investment, high-reward ventures that bring the brand closer to the consumer. Understanding the essence of this ever-evolving phenomenon is imperative to any business aiming to lead in this dynamic retail landscape.

As we journey further into this report, we'll guide you through various critical aspects of setting up a successful pop-up store, including choosing the right location, creating an immersive customer experience, leveraging marketing strategies, and finally, measuring the success of your pop-up venture.

Chapter 3. The Pros and Cons of Temporary Retail

The flourishing of pop-up retail ventures is no coincidence; it is a strategic response to the shifting dynamics of the retail arena, challenged by online e-commerce platforms and the ever-evolving consumer behavior. However, as with any venture, starting a temporary retail store comes with its fair share of benefits and challenges. Grasping these nuances enriches our understanding of the pop-up world and assists in determining if this retail approach is suitable for your entrepreneurial aspirations.

3.1. Understanding the Appeal of Pop-up Stores

The empirical growth of pop-up stores is mostly attributed to their incredibly appealing characteristics. They offer a low-risk, high-reward opportunity for both budding and seasoned entrepreneurs.

1. *Affordability*: A significant advantage is the low startup cost compared to traditional retailing. Limited timeframe results in reduced lease expenses. Besides, the flexible nature of these stores allows for minimal and cost-effective setups.

2. *Test the Market*: A pop-up store acts as a live lab for brands to experiment with new products, marketing strategies, and locations. They can gather essential real-time feedback and gauge customer receptivity without significant investment.

3. *Brand Awareness*: Pop-up shops infuse a sense of urgency and exclusivity that attracts customers, thereby increasing visibility and generating buzz around your brand.

4. *Engaging Customer Experiences*: Strategically designed pop-up stores can offer unique, immersive experiences, profoundly

enhancing brand engagement and loyalty.

5. *Inventory Liquidation*: For businesses looking to efficiently liquidate excess or seasonal stock, pop-up shops can come in quite handy.

3.2. The Hurdles in the Pop-up Retail Landscape

Despite their inherent charm, pop-up stores come with their own set of challenges. Understanding these will help entrepreneurs navigate better and strategize effectively.

1. *Limited Timeframe*: While the brevity of pop-up shops can be a boon, it can also manifest as a challenge. Building brand recognition and a loyal customer base within such a short timeframe can be demanding.

2. *Operational Challenges*: Quick setup and takedown of the store, along with logistic issues such as sourcing, stocking, and staffing, can be a daunting task, particularly for retail novices.

3. *Regulatory Hurdles*: Temporary businesses are often subject to a different set of regulations than traditional businesses, including licensing and permits, which vary significantly by location.

4. *Rent Negotiation*: While lower leasing cost is an attraction, determining the acceptable lease amount and negotiating it can be complex due to lack of benchmark prices for temporary leases.

5. *Customer Retention*: Maintaining the customer base after the pop-up store closes can be challenging, primarily if not complemented with robust online presence or other physical stores.

3.3. Mastering the Art of Pop-up Retail: Practical Tips

While the pros and cons provide a clear picture of what to expect, these practical tips equip you with the tools required to make your pop-up store a smashing success.

1. *Unique Concept*: To stand out in the competitive landscape, your store needs a unique theme, story, or product that could excite the target customers.

2. *Location, Location, Location*: Setting up in a high footfall area or a location that aligns with the brand identity can drastically improve visibility and customer engagement.

3. *Integrated Marketing Approach*: Use of multiple communication channels, from social media to print advertising, is crucial for capturing diverse audience segments.

4. *Exceptional Customer Service*: Ensuring a delightful customer experience not only boosts sales but also increases the chances of customers promoting your brand through word-of-mouth.

5. *Planning and Implementation*: Last but not least, meticulous planning followed by efficient execution is required to curb any operational challenges.

In conclusion, pop-up stores offer an excellent avenue for venturing into retail without shouldering the typical financial or operational burdens associated with traditional retail settings. While the endeavor comes with its difficulties, the potential return on investment and the opportunity to deeply engage with customers make it an exciting choice for many entrepreneurs. By understanding and addressing the challenges head-on, temporary retail can be turned into a valuable asset in your retail strategy.

Whether you're a nascent entrepreneur or an established brand, knowing the pros, cons, and some effective strategies can enable you to harness the potential of pop-up retail, fostering a business venture that not only delights your customers but also substantially improves your bottom line.

Chapter 4. Unpacking Your Unique Selling Proposition

Before we explore the depths of how one can unpack the unique selling proposition (USP) of their pop-up store, it's critical to understand what USP is. Universally accepted across marketing and sales sectors, USP is the one thing that separates your product, service, or in this case, your pop-up store from the next. It's the unique quality that gives your business an edge over others. With understanding comes vision, and with vision comes the ability to create something unique. When your pop-up store has a persuasive USP, it invariably draws customers towards itself more confidently, and that's magical for your temporary store. So, let's delve into the art of unpacking your Unique Selling Proposition.

4.1. Defining Your USP

Start by identifying what truly sets your pop-up shop apart from others. To do this, consider your target audience, their needs, desires, and how your product or service caters to them uniquely. Are you selling ethically sourced products, giving consumers peace of mind? Or perhaps you're offering a techie wonderland, where customers can interact with the latest gadgets in a comfortable, home-like setting? The possibilities are endless. Salient aspects of your USP could be numerous, ranging from product quality, price, location, experience, or even your story. It is up to you to identify and articulate it.

4.2. Understanding Your Market

To hone in on your USP, you'll need a deep comprehension of your market. Break down your industry to understand customer behaviour and identify gaps that you can fill. Employ market research, conduct surveys, enrol in consumer focus groups and consult experts in the retail space. The more information you gather, the clearer your brand vision becomes which, in turn, crystallizes your USP.

4.3. Evaluating Your Competitors

A critical step to unlocking your USP involves in-depth competitor analysis. Look at other pop-up stores or similar retail businesses: what do they promise their customers? What do you do differently, or better? If you can pinpoint where they're falling short, or areas where you shine, you can structure your USP around it, making it a compelling hook for customers to choose you over others.

4.4. The Brand Story

Your brand story can be a significant part of your USP. A narrative around your brand, telling how, why, and who started the pop-up shop, can create an emotional connection with the customers. By adding this element, your pop-up shop differentiates itself. It's not just about what you're selling; it's about giving customers a reason to buy from you. Everyone loves a good story.

4.5. Crafting Your USP: Distilling The Essence

When it's time to express your USP, remember to keep it clear, concise, and easy to understand. It's tempting to include details about every single feature and benefit that sets you apart, but this may end up confusing your customers. The trick is to distill your USP down to its essence. Simplicity is the name of the game.

4.6. Testing Your USP

Once you have a potential USP in sight, test it. Share it with close friends and colleagues whose opinions you trust. You can also conduct A/B testing using digital platforms like social media or email marketing - use different iterations of your USP and see which brings better engagement.

4.7. Communicating Your USP

An effective USP must be communicated and expressed consistently across all customer touchpoints – your website, brochures, advertisements, and most importantly, your pop-up store. It should reflect in your décor, staff interactions, product packaging and more. The objective is to ensure that your USP is ingrained in the customer's mind whenever they interact with your brand.

Unpacking your Unique Selling Proposition involves a lot of introspection, market understanding, competitor analysis, and intuitive leap of faith. It's your secret sauce. However, remember that your USP may evolve with time and that's okay. The market is dynamic and so should be your business approach. Be open to continuous learning and improvement. Embrace this exciting journey of pop-up retailing with all its challenges and rewards, and you'd soon witness retail magic unfold!

Chapter 5. Strategic Planning: Location, Timing, and Presentation

Choosing the right location, timing, and presentation style for your pop-up shop can determine its success. These strategic decisions serve as crucial stepping stones in your business venture. Let's dive into each of these elements to understand their importance and establish effective strategies for each.

5.1. Location: Finding the Perfect Spot

The location of the pop-up shop is fundamental to attracting the right audience and foot traffic. A good location increases brand visibility and drives sales. Therefore, it's essential to scout for potential premises meticulously.

5.1.1. Understanding Your Target Market

Before going location-hunting, entrepreneurs must understand their target market, as this will significantly influence the choice of location. Think about your ideal customer: where do they live, hang out, and shop? After collecting this data, choose a location that allows your target market to easily find and visit the shop.

5.1.2. High Traffic Locations

High traffic or popular locations immediately gain attention, leading to potential customer discovery and engagement. Such locations can be in or near shopping malls, busy streets, festival sites or fairgrounds, and other crowded areas.

5.1.3. Consider the Expenses

While a prime location might promise exciting opportunities, entrepreneurs must consider the cost. Initial investment, rental fees, transportation, utilities, or necessary shop setup costs - hidden or otherwise - should all be part of the decision-making.

5.2. Timing: Seizing the Right Moment

The perfect timing for launching your pop-up shop plays a significant role in your shop's success. It could be influenced by factors such as holidays, seasons, and events.

5.2.1. Season-based Popup Shops

Seasons and holidays provide excellent opportunities for pop-up shops – Christmas, summer, and Halloween, to name a few. Schedule your pop-up shop to coincide with these seasons, and offer products or services related to the theme.

5.2.2. Timing with Events

Launching a pop-up shop at the time of local festivals, concerts, or a community event can guarantee high footfall and increased engagement.

5.2.3. Market Trends

Staying updated on current market trends is vital. Keep an eye on emerging trends that align with your offerings and plan your pop-up shop accordingly.

5.3. Presentation: Crafting a Unique Experience

The presentation of your shop will dictate how customers perceive and remember your brand. Create an environment that is unique, visually pleasing, and engaging.

5.3.1. Visual Merchandising

Use visual merchandising strategies to attract and entertain shoppers. A well-designed window display can pull people in, while the creative arrangement of products inside can increase the chance of a sale.

5.3.2. Engaging Store Layout

The layout of your store can influence the customer's journey. Consider factors such as aisles width, product placement, and checkout location. Have strategic and engaging signage to guide and persuade customers.

5.3.3. Personalized Engagement

Find ways to engage with your customers personally. Be it creating Instagram-worthy spots or interactive displays that provide a unique shopping experience, or offering personalized solutions, engaging your customers will leave a lasting impression.

In conclusion, strategic planning in location, timing, and presentation can accelerate your pop-up store's success. Consider each factor in detail while planning, and never ignore customer's needs and preferences. The right blend of these elements would potentially unlock the door to a successful pop-up shop venture, leaving your competitors wondering how you did it.

Chapter 6. Building A Captivating Brand for a Short-Lived Shop

Building a captivating brand for a short-lived shop isn't just about presenting attractive commodities. It involves building a narrative around your products that connects with your target audience on an emotional level. The more they resonate with your brand's story and ideals, the more likely they are to patronize your pop-up store. Let's start this journey by understanding what exactly brand building involves.

6.1. Brand Building: What it Means and Why it Matters

Brand building involves creating a distinct and recognizable identity for your shop that encapsulates the values, tenets, and promises that your business stands for. This identity should speak volumes about what your shop offers and why customers should choose you over other retailers. For a pop-up shop, a strong brand image can make all the difference, setting it apart from competitors and helping customers remember it long after it's gone.

Your brand identity should be communicated consistently across all elements connected to your shop — from your shop decor to your staff uniforms, product packaging, promotions, and even how you respond to customer inquiries. Each element must reinforce your brand's persona and create a seamless shopping experience.

6.2. Crafting Your Brand Story

In order to create an engaging brand, you must first have a compelling brand story. The brand story encapsulates how your pop-up shop came to be, what it seeks to accomplish, and how it plans to improve its customers' lives. It's more than just a sequence of events; it's an emotional journey that can stir individuals and motivate them to be a part of your business's story.

When designing your brand story, ponder over these questions: Why did you launch your pop-up store? What makes your shop unique? How does your shop make the lives of your customers better? These narratives frame your brand's essence and provide a background that helps to distinguish your shop from others.

Remember, people connect with stories, not facts and figures. Utilize storytelling techniques to ensure your brand story is engaging, memorable, and authentic. Incorporate real-life experiences, challenges, and triumphs that led to the inception of your pop-up store. Your brand story should inspire, resonate with your target market, and be a testament to what your brand stands for.

6.3. Building a Brand Personality

A captivating brand isn't just known; it's recognizable by traits that mirror a personality. Just as a person is identified by qualities such as friendly, dependable, pioneering, or sophisticated, your brand too, should have clearly identifiable qualities. Establishing a brand personality helps give your pop-up store a unique identity, making it more relatable to your customers.

Start by identifying who your target audience is. What are their interests, habits, and needs? From there, craft a brand personality that appeals to them. Is your audience young, trend-savvy individuals? A vibrant, daring, and innovative brand personality could appeal to them. Arc they environmentally aware? Adopting a sustainable, eco-friendly brand personality may resonate more.

6.4. The Power of Visual Identity

Branding extends beyond narratives and personalities. Visual branding plays a crucial role in building a captivating brand for your pop-up store. Your logo, color scheme, typography, decor and store layout, merchandise display, packaging — everything should reflect your brand personality and story.

An effective visual identity is one that is distinctive and consistent. It should be visually harmonious across all platforms, whether it be in-store displays, social media, or promotional materials. Bear in mind that you will have only a short span to impress potential customers in a pop-up setting — a compelling and visually consistent branding can attract and imprint on your customers' minds.

6.5. Letting Your Brand Live

The last and critical step is actualizing your brand. Solidify your brand's presence in the minds of your customers through touchpoints like websites, social media, email marketing, and more. Be proactive in your brand communication strategies and show them that your brand exists not only to sell a product but to improve their lifestyle in some way.

Be open to feedback and dialogue with your customers. Show them that their opinions matter and that you're willing to improve based on their needs. This breeds loyalty, turning one-off customers into brand advocates, contributing to your pop-up store's success.

Remember, a pop-up shop is an experience, and your brand is the soul of that experience. By focusing on these aspects of brand building, you can create a captivating, emotionally resonant brand that would ensure your pop-up shop is not just temporary — it's memorable.

Chapter 7. Clever Marketing Tactics for Maximum Exposure

Creating visibility for your pop-up store is pivotal to its success. Without effective marketing strategies, even the most innovative and well-stocked pop-up store might flounder in obscurity. This chapter delves deep into the world of marketing, outlining tactics and approaches to help your pop-up store achieve maximum exposure.

7.1. Crafting a Unique Brand Identity

First and foremost, create a distinct identity for your pop-up store. The temporary nature of these ventures shouldn't detract from their character and appeal. To compete with established retail players, devise an original and consistently applied visual narrative.

Distinguish your pop-up store with a unique name, logo, color scheme, typography, and photography style. Every detail blends to evoke an emotional response from your potential customers, which subsequently drives brand recall and loyalty.

7.2. Leveraging Social Media

Social media platforms are your allies. They offer affordable, wide-reaching, and versatile channels to connect with your target audience effectively. Use a variety of platforms - Instagram, Facebook, Twitter, LinkedIn, Pinterest, and TikTok, each with unique strengths.

Instagram, with its focus on visuals, suits aesthetically pleasing products or themed pop-up stores. Twitter, a platform of conversation and trending topics, can make your brand part of the daily chatter. Pinterest shines for inspiration - think fashion, decor, and DIY projects. Each platform presents opportunities to engage your audience and build visibility through shareable, entertaining, and informative content.

7.3. Harnessing Influencer Partnerships

Influencer marketing is a powerful tool for pop-up stores. By partnering with influencers relevant to your niche, you can leverage their existing audience. This approach lends credibility to your brand as the influencer's endorsement acts as a form of social proof, which helps to drive traffic and sales.

When choosing influencers, focus not only on their follower count but also engagement rate—those with a highly engaged community will yield more results than those with passive large followings.

7.4. Creating Buzz with Events

Events, both online and offline, draw attention to your pop-up store. You can create buzz even before your doors are formally open with "sneak peek" events, early bird offers, or a countdown on your website or social media channels.

An exclusive launch event can attract influencers, bloggers, and journalists who will cover the event, thereby further promoting your brand. A series of in-store events throughout your pop-up's tenure, such as workshops, meet-the-maker sessions, or theme days, maintains momentum and adds a dynamic element to your brand's story.

7.5. Tailoring an SEO Strategy

A well-executed Search Engine Optimization (SEO) strategy can improve your visibility online. Start by identifying the keywords your target market uses when searching for products or services similar to yours. Integrate these keywords strategically in your website content, blog posts, product descriptions, meta tags, and alt image text.

Area-specific keywords are especially important if your pop-up store is targeting a specific geographic market. Ensure that your store's location is clear across your online content to gain visibility among potential local customers.

7.6. Utilizing Email Marketing

Despite the social media boom, email marketing retains its value. It provides a direct line of communication with your customers and allows for personalized engagement.

Capture email addresses by offering incentives like promotional offers or exclusive information. Keep your audience engaged with regular updates, including new product information, events, special offers, and any exciting news related to your pop-up store.

7.7. Engaging Traditional Media

While digital marketing forms the bulk of modern strategies, traditional media outlets still hold considerable influence. Reach out to local newspapers, regional TV stations, and relevant magazines. A well-placed article or feature can significantly boost your pop-up store's visibility.

Creating a press release with key information about your unique selling propositions, high-quality images, quotes from the founders or designers, and clear contact details provides interested journalists with an easy-to-use package of information.

7.8. Involving the Community

Pop-up stores thrive on the sense of impermanence and novelty they inspire. Tap into local communities, resident associations, and local events for a mutual promotion. Engage with the community not just as consumers, but as participants in the unique retail experience you are offering.

In conclusion, visibility and buzz for your pop-up store are achievable with a mix of traditional and modern marketing tactics. Shape your message carefully and choose channels fitting your brand and target demographic. The goal is to create a captivating narrative around your pop-up store, one that intrigues and invites customers to be a part of your temporary retail adventure.

Chapter 8. Optimizing Social Media for Your Pop-Up Business

Understanding the weight social media has on contemporary business models is imperative when starting your pop-up shop. Not only is this a platform that offers wide exposure, but also a platform that creates customer engagement and fosters relationships, ultimately adding to the pop-up shop's experience and memory in the consumer's mind.

8.1. Defining Your Social Media Goals

When it comes to social media marketing, a catch-all approach will not suffice. Define your business goals first, and determine how social media can facilitate these objectives. Possibilities are endless: spreading brand awareness, driving traffic to your website, promoting a special promotion or event, increasing product sales, and building a loyal community. Determine which results you need and create strategies emphasizing these goals for each relevant social media platform.

8.2. Choosing the Right Platforms

Understanding where your target demographic spends their time online is necessary to ensure your social media efforts are directed towards the most relevant channels. The visually appealing nature of pop-up shops means Instagram, with its focus on visual content, could be a suitable choice. If promoting a pop-up shop event, Facebook gives options for creating event pages and inviting followers. Twitter, on the other hand, could be beneficial for short, frequent updates about the shop's location or stock.

8.3. Developing a Cohesive Brand Identity

A consistent brand identity across all social media platforms can lead to increased recognition and an overall stronger brand presence. This includes a consistent voice, visuals, and messaging across all networks to build trust and familiarity with your audience. Develop a branding guide that outlines your company's mission, values, color palette, typography, tone of voice, and personality. This will ensure uniformity in all communication and promotional activities.

8.4. Creating Valuable Content

Content is at the heart of any social media strategy. Thus, the content you share should be valuable to your audience, engage them, and prompt them to action. Alternate between different content types – from behind-the-scenes snapshots to customer testimonials, product highlights to influencer shout-outs. Additionally, leveraging user-generated content is a robust way of enhancing authenticity and trust.

8.5. Harnessing User-Generated Content

User-generated content (UGC) transforms your customers into your marketers and is particularly effective for pop-up shops, which rely on word-of-mouth publicity. Encourage visitors to your pop-up store to share their experiences, upload photos, mention your brand, or use specific hashtags. Frequently share such content on your own profiles to provide social proof.

8.6. Engaging with Your Community

Building a community around your pop-up shop is vital for creating buzz and driving traffic. The more you interact, the more engaged your audience will feel. Respond to comments, ask for feedback, answer queries promptly, and start conversations. Use platforms like Instagram and Facebook to host contests, giveaways, and polls. Broadcast live Q&A sessions, seminars, or tours of your pop-up shop.

8.7. Utilizing Influencer Partnerships

Influencers command large, engaged audiences and can play a significant role in your social media strategy. Connect with influencers fitting your brand's persona and values. Organize influencer meet-ups at your pop-up shop and encourage them to post about their experience. Micro-influencers, having a smaller but more engaged audience, can play a significant role in driving local traffic to your store.

8.8. Measuring Success

Identify key performance indicators (KPIs) to understand whether your social media strategy is working. These could be follower growth rate, engagement rate, click-through rate, conversions, or the number of user-generated posts. Make use of social media analytics tools for tracking these KPIs and use this data to iterate and improve your strategy.

Implementing a comprehensive social media strategy will not only rocket your pop-up shop into the limelight but will also fortify your brand's overall presence in the dynamic and evolving retail landscape. This foundation will play a pivotal role in the overall success of your pop-up business.

Chapter 9. Avoiding Common Pitfalls in Temporary Retail

Starting a temporary retail shop comes with a long list of pros, such as the potential for increased brand awareness and revenue, as well as the opportunity to test the market. However, diving headfirst into any new business endeavor inevitably brings its share of risks. Awareness of the common pitfalls in this sector can help you steer clear of them and ensure that your business survives even in a brisk and buoyant climate like the world of pop-up stores.

9.1. Understanding the Importance of Location

Location should be the cornerstone of your pop-up shop strategy. The wrong location can deflate your store's footfall and revenues rapidly. Analyze the demographics, the hustle and bustle, the norms and nuances of your intended locality before making a move.

Ensure your shop is easily accessible and in the public eye. Popular spaces are shopping malls, high streets, festivals, and markets. Standalone pop-ups might attract curiosity, but if they are inconvenient for customers to find, they will not gain the desired traction. So, while creativity in location choice is appreciated, convenience and visibility should never be compromised.

9.2. Mastering the Lease Negotiations

Leasing temporary retail space could be a challenging task. Unlike traditional retailers with long-term leases, pop-ups operate on short-term agreements. Landlords might demand higher rent due to the short-term nature of the lease. Always negotiate and try to find a win-win agreement. Understand your rights as a tenant, read your lease carefully, and get expert advice if you feel out of your depth.

Don't just focus on rent costs. Other expenses like utilities, insurance, and upkeep can add significantly to your overheads. Remember to account for these costs in your budget and try to negotiate shared costs with your landlord, if possible.

9.3. Nailing the Visual Merchandising

The way you present your products and your store layout can have a massive impact on your sales. In the case of pop-ups, first impressions matter even more as the customer doesn't have a clear expectation of your brand yet.

Create a planogram - a visual representation of the store layout - before setting up shop. This not only simplifies the process but also helps you visualize the customer flow. Place the products strategically - high selling items at eye level, impulse goods near the checkout area, and high-value items in locked displays.

Remember, pop-up shops are not traditional stores. They are usually smaller, and creating a memorable and engaging customer experience is key.

9.4. Budgeting and Financial Projections

A common pitfall in temporary retail is to underestimate the required budget. Set up costs, inventory purchase, staff wages, utilities, and marketing expensess can increase rapidly.

Develop a detailed financial plan. Realistic revenue projections are as important as budgeting. Understand your sales cycle - will you sell more on weekdays or weekends? Do seasons affect your sales? Once you understand these aspects, you can create detailed daily sales projections.

Keeping track of your actual performance against your projections will help you identify trends, adapt, and navigate the financial landscape of your pop-up better.

9.5. Hiring and Staffing

Unlike traditional retail stores, pop-ups usually operate on a lean staff model. However, hiring the right number and the right kind of staff is crucial. Your team should not only be sales-savvy but also able to deliver an exceptional customer experience in line with your brand image.

Hiring temporary staff could pose issues. Make sure to provide ample training and create a strong work ethic. A dedicated staff that is passionate about the product and the brand can convert one-time customers into regular ones.

9.6. Managing Inventory

Inventory management is a crucial aspect of your pop-up shop's operations. Having too little inventory could result in lost sales, but too much inventory entails tying up your capital and risking increased costs due to unsold goods.

Develop a systematic inventory management system. Keep track of your product's life cycle and delve into the world of forecasting techniques to predict future demand. If possible, use technology like Point-of-Sale (POS) systems to get real-time inventory status and sales data.

9.7. Branding and Marketing

While pop-up shops inherently possess word-of-mouth potential because of their unique and ephemeral nature, relying solely on this would be a mistake.

Invest time and resources to create a strong marketing strategy - a poorly marketed pop-up store is a business opportunity squandered. Utilize digital marketing channels - social media, email marketing, SEO, and influencers - to hype up your audience in the days preceding the pop-up. Traditional forms of publicity, like local newspapers and radio, can also be effective.

Remember, the return on investment for marketing can be hard to calculate, but it is vital.

9.8. Legal Aspects

Ensure that you thoroughly understand the laws and regulations related to pop-up stores in your location. These might include business licenses, health and safety norms, food and safety permits (if you are selling edible items), and insurance.

Ensure that all contracts with suppliers, landlords, and staff are legally sound. Retain a lawyer if needed, as ignoring legal aspects can result in costly lawsuits and penalties.

These potential pitfalls should not deter your entrepreneurial spirit. Instead, consider these as stepping stones to your pop-up store's success. With careful planning and strategic thinking, these common pitfalls can be avoided, and your temporary retail venture can truly thrive.

Chapter 10. Funding Your Dream Pop-Up Shop: Budgeting and Expenses

Understanding the financial landscape of a pop-up store is crucial. It's the fuel that propels your dream from a mere concept into a physical reality. When mapping out your financial journey, you need to consider budgeting, expenses, and securing sufficient funding.

10.1. Budgeting for Your Pop-Up Store

Crafting an effective budget is pivotal to the success of your pop-up store. The budgeting process sets the essential framework that enables you to assess financial viability, forecasting revenues and anticipating costs.

10.1.1. Forecasting Revenue

Determining your pop-up store's potential revenue might be challenging due to the temporary nature of the business, possible seasonal fluctuations, and unknown consumer responses. Yet, it is fundamental. Basis for revenue forecasting can be gathered from similar businesses, online analytics, or initial test sales. Estimating conservatively offers a more realistic outlook and helps you plan for the worst while hoping for the best.

- Market analysis: Identify and analyze similar pop-up stores, their prices, and sales volume.

- Online analytics: Analyze trends in keyword searches, online traffic, and social media engagement for products similar to your offering.

- Test sales: Pre-launch sales can inform potential consumer interest and willingness to buy.

10.1.2. Anticipating Costs

The heart and soul of budgeting happen when drafting the cost side. Costs for a pop-up store are typically lower than long-term retail spaces, but they still require diligent planning and attention. They should be classified as fixed and variable costs.

- Fixed costs: These are expenses incurred regardless of sales volume. Examples entail rent, utilities, insurance, salaries for permanent staff, and marketing.

- Variable costs: These costs change with the volume of sales. This includes the cost of goods sold (COGS), shipping, packaging, and wages for temporary staff.

10.2. Securing Funding

After drafting a detailed budget, you will have a clearer idea about the necessary starting capital. Several avenues are available when seeking financial backing for your pop-up store.

10.2.1. Personal Savings

Self-financing your pop-up dream is the quickest and most painless option, assuming you have the necessary funding comfortably available. It eliminates the hassle and expenses associated with loans or investor hunting.

- Savings: If you've been lucky enough to build a nest egg over time, consider this as a reliable source.

- Retirement funds: Tread cautiously here. Draining your

retirement savings could bring significant repercussions down the line.

10.2.2. Bank Loans

Should personal finance be unavailable or insufficient, a business loan from a renowned bank or credit union can be a practical choice. To secure a loan, a concrete business plan, solid credit history, and possible collateral may be required.

- Business loan: Traditional banking institutions offer funding with varying interest rates and repayment terms. These can be either secured (backed with collateral) or unsecured.

- Line of credit: For flexible financing, seeking a business line of credit can give you access to funds up to a certain limit.

10.2.3. Crowdfunding and Alternative Financing

Crowdfunding is a viable resource, the success of which heavily depends on your ability to create an enticing campaign. Other niche options are also available like merchant cash advances or trade-credit.

- Crowdfunding: Platforms like Kickstarter and Indiegogo enable people worldwide to invest in your idea in return for rewards.

- Merchant cash advance: Businesses receive upfront cash in exchange for a portion of future sales.

- Trade credit: An agreement where suppliers allow you to pay for goods or services at a later date.

10.3. Managing Expenses

Vigilant expense management is key for ensuring viability and profitability. Tracking and reviewing your expenses regularly enables you to stay in control and make necessary adjustments if required.

10.3.1. Record Keeping

Maintain receipts of all transactions to develop a healthy financial record. Use software like QuickBooks or Xero for easy cataloging and tracking.

10.3.2. Regular Review

Perform regular financial health checks. Compare actual versus budgeted costs to identify areas of improvement.

10.3.3. Cost Saving and Negotiation

Always look for ways to reduce costs without compromising the quality of your goods or services. Consider negotiation with suppliers for better terms.

To conclude, funding your dream pop-up shop is a journey filled with practicalities, risks, excitement, and significant potential rewards. It is a process that demands attention to detail, adept financial skills, and a solid grasp on budgeting and expenses. The key is awareness - you must understand where every dollar is coming from and where it's destined to go. Accomplishing this can help make the dream of your pop-up store a tangible, thriving reality.

Chapter 11. Case Studies: Successful Pop-Up Retailers' Strategies

Kick-starting this enlightening journey, let's immerse ourselves in the well-crafted strategies of successful pop-up retailers. This exploration will furnish us with a detailed understanding of how these entrepreneurs transformed their fleeting stores into something memorable, engaging, and profitable.

11.1. Unconventional Location: 'The Street Store'

Playing ingeniously on the concept of a charitable pop-up, \"The Street Store\" adopted a unique business strategy to serve the homeless. The team didn't venture for a traditional brick-and-mortar building but opted for an open sidewalk. Their target customers were people without a home with an immediate need for clothing and essentials. With hangers made of cardboard, they created a pop-up store that catered to this population's immediate needs. Moreover, they invited the local community to donate, which resulted in a fantastic response.

The brand quickly gained recognition and support, creating a profound social impact. This extraordinary move showcases a canny understanding of their client base and how an unconventional, heartfelt approach can resonate deeply with customers and communities alike.

11.2. Experiential Retail: 'Target's Dollhouse'

Recognizing the looming potential of experiential retail, Target chose a daringly creative approach. In 2013, they set up a life-sized, 2-storey dollhouse in Grand Central Terminal, New York. The dollhouse was equipped with 3500 different items from their new collection of home furnishings, aptly named "Threshold."

Visitors could explore and interact with the products in a homely setting. This immersive experience made the customers feel as if they were walking inside a home décor catalog. Target's strategy shows how a well-thought-out immersive environment can encourage customer engagement and increase product awareness.

11.3. Limited-Edition Products: 'Snapchat Spectacles'

In 2016, Snapchat astounded fans with its pop-up shop in New York City. They sold their new product, "Snapchat Spectacles", exclusively from bright yellow vending machines known as Snapbots. The surprise release of the limited-edition products created a buzz. Fans lined up for hours to get their hands on these products, creating impressive media coverage.

Snapchat's strategy displayed how scarcity and exclusivity can stimulate demand and induce a sense of urgency in consumers, pushing them to buy.

11.4. Dining with a Difference: 'P.F. Chang's Lettuce Wrap Pop-up'

P.F. Chang's orchestrated their strategy perfectly when they launched a one-day lettuce wrap pop-up in Soho Square, London, in 2019. The pop-up exclusively served lettuce wraps made-to-order for people around the area and was a smashing success.

P.F. Chang's core strategy was to create awareness about their iconic lettuce wraps while building excitement for their upcoming London restaurant opening. They ensured customer engagement by experimenting with varied offerings and ensured product awareness through firsthand experience.

11.5. An Escape from the Mundane: 'IKEA Play Café'

IKEA Play Café was much more than a regular pop-up shop in Toronto in 2017. This concept consisted of a unique blend of a showroom, shop, and café and aimed to provide an interactive and fun experience to IKEA customers.

The Play Café offered food, games, and displayed IKEA products in unique lifestyle settings. The strategy at play here was diversification, aiming to appeal to a wide customer base and provide them with a memorable experience distinct from the classic IKEA shopping trip.

Each of these case studies underscores unique business strategies, proving that the pivot to pop-up retail stores is not trend-based but a valuable and viable venture. These are just a few examples of the multitude of ways entrepreneurs can channel creativity into unconventional retail strategies, highlighting the exciting potentialities of the pop-up arena.

The diverse approach these brands took, from focusing on social causes, creating experiential retail moments, to product scarcity, underscores the limitless freedom the business model provides. Approach your strategy with creativity, audacity, and thoughtful planning; who knows, your pop-up shop might be our next case study!